What O...

I met Cathy in a coffee shop. Go figure! (I bet a whole mess of us can say that!) On my breaks or when customers were nil, I'd sit with her and drink in her immense love of the Word. Scriptures rolled off her tongue and were surrounded with an incredible warmness. I knew she was the real deal! Cathy knows the Word of God and makes it her aim to live it out. It's evident by her service and gracious living, meaning that she lays down her life for others. Her book, "Letters from a Mother's Heart" speaks loudly of this, encouraging us to live other-world, the opposite of how the world would advise us to live. She has a profound way of stirring up a great hunger (in myself and others) to know the Word.

I'm honored and humbled to have her in my life, modeling Christ's love!

Ellie Hale
Rancher Wife and Homeschool Mom

I loved receiving these letters from Cathy. As a mother of young children that outnumber me, it's very obvious to me that I need all the help I can get-- especially priceless wisdom shared from willing mothers who have gone before me. What Cathy shares is relatable and practical, and reminds me to always go back to the giver of wisdom and the word. Because of her instruction, I have memorized verses and made better reading habits that have a big impact on daily life for the whole family. I feel there is a lot of information out there about raising children and how you want them to turn out, but I haven't seen much tried-and-true "this is how you get there" advice. And this is why I feel like this will be so valuable to whomever is privileged to read it.

Now I look forward to the future (of at least three teenagers) with a little less trepidation!

Stephanie Westley Chayrez
Mom of daughters and to twins

I wanted you to know that your letters are very encouraging to me, helping me to refocus on what is important, and reminding me to look to my Lord and God and Savior Jesus Christ for strength and guidance, rather than relying on myself for the good that comes from God alone...Thank you, my dear, for sharing your experiences with those of us who are bonded to each other through the love of our children and of God.

Mona
Mom, Pastor, Teacher

God designed us to need each other. In true Titus 2:3-4 fashion, Cathy Horning mentors moms by sharing her heart in sixteen letters. Her mom wisdom is dispensed in a relateable and informal way. The short and to the point messages tackle the typical concerns and struggles most moms have. The insights given are born from experience, faith in the Lord, and love for family. With humility, Cathy reflects and gently challenges the reader to be the mom God created her to be. Letter's From a Mother's Heart will bless yours.

Lori Wildenberg
Mom, Author of 5 Parenting Books, Speaker and Parent Coach; www.loriwildenberg.com

A must-have for every mom! Using biblical wisdom and practical teachings, Cathy Horning shows how you can make a lasting difference in your child's life through letters filled with wisdom and encourage-ment. These letters will inspire and equip you to intentionally embrace the ministry of motherhood.

Heather Riggleman
Speaker, Blogger, Grace Dweller, Mom, Award-winning Journalist and Author of Mama Needs a Time Out

I have moments of great despair, frustration, and, yes, anger. I continue to pray for patience and strength as I continue to learn (from my children). Your letters remind me, I am human! They also bring biblical passages new meaning and refreshing enlightenment.

Carolyn
Special Needs Mom

I have thoroughly enjoyed your letters. Keep up the awesome ministry.

Mandy
Mom

I just received your latest letter! It was so good. A wealth of information. Your love for the Lord always comes through. And your love for your children is always so refreshing. God has shown you so much in parenting your children. I'm so encouraged by your obedience. I love and appreciate you Cathy.

Jodie
Military Mom

I have 5 children, and your letters have been a blessing and an encouragement.

Bonnie
Mom to many

Letters from a Mother's Heart

Timeless Truths From One Mom's Journey

Cathy E. Horning

Letters from a Mother's Heart
By Cathy E. Horning
www.cathyhorning.com
Email: cathy@cathyhorning.com

Published by In Step Publishing
Copyright ©2018 by In Step Publishing

Layout and Design by: ChristianAuthorsGetPaid.com
Cover Designed by Benji Horning
Cover Photo by Dana Ryan Photography
Edited by Katie Horning
Artwork by Katie Horning

DISCLAIMER

Every person sees the same, exact story a little differently. Therefore, the writing and now retelling of these stories and letters are from the author's personal perspective and her best recollection, and she has made every effort to relay any details as accurately as possible. Speaking from her many years of tears, prayers, successes, failures, and experiences, the tips and ideas contained herein represent her personal opinions and recommendations. Although the author believes her advice to be sound, she does not assume any liability for any loss, risk, or injury incurred by individuals who read or act on the information enclosed. Each reader must carefully weigh any and all aspects of any personal decision before making any changes in his or her life.

Printed in the United States of America

ISBN 978-0692986295

Dedication

To you, dear Mama!

May these letters encourage you, as you seek to train up your children in the way God uniquely created them to go, and point you to the race He has marked out for you and your family to run with perseverance. (Hebrews 12:1) *Fixing our eyes on Jesus the author and perfector of our faith, who for the joy set before Him endured the cross. Heb 12:2*

Dearest Julie,

Thank you for being my faithful role model, mentor and praying friend! I love you so very much!

Cathy ♡

Acknowledgements

To my Abba Father, my dear Lord Jesus, and the relentless Spirit Helper who patiently taught me to become the mom I longed to be. And, who birthed the seeds for this book in my heart, long before it would be published.

To Kathleen D. Mailer, of Christian Writers Get Paid, who, in God's perfect timing, personally and passionately fanned the spark in me to finally get my book written.

To my amazing children, Daniel, Benji, Katie, and Dustin, who challenged me to grow, forgave me when I blew it (over and over again), and loved me through it all. They, and their spouses, have supported me in so many ways, including the publishing of this book. Thank you for letting me share our stories. I love you!

To my remarkable husband, who has always seen within me things I could not see in myself. Who loved me, supported me, prayed for me, led and modeled to me wise and great parenting. I love you babe!

To my mentors and mom friends, thank you for loving me through it all. Thank you for weathering the parenting journey by my side. As an introvert mommy, who tended to keep my roots from going too deep, I am so grateful for those who stuck with me, prayed for me, modeled to me (I was watching you), gave me breaks, and loved me and my kids on the mountain tops and in the valleys!

Table of Contents

Foreword

Who knew that one shared wedding dress would lead to a lifetime of friendship? 36 years ago a sweet girl had need of a wedding dress and as I had just given birth to my first born I knew I was not going to be using my wedding dress any time soon. I gladly lent my dress to a woman I had met once because my mom let me know her need and I was more than happy to see my dress used again. As a bride, this woman looked stunning. Thus began the thirty-six years long unlikely friendship.

She was the calm to my crazy, the sweet to my spicy, the quiet to my loud from my mouth to my clothes. She and I could not have been more opposite and yet God in his wisdom and humor knew we needed each other desperately. Our lives paralleled through our years as friends. If I did not love her and know God was involved, I would say we were in a competition to copy one another.

My first son was followed by her first son, my second son by her second son. My daughter then her daughter with my last born amazing son followed by

1

her caboose of an amazing son. The fact even our 10 plus grandchildren are stair stepped in a similar fashion is evidence of the how intertwined our lives are.

Throughout the years, Cathy has been a voice of reason to the stressed out, worn out momma's heart. Many a day we would sit at each other's kitchen tables, talking, whining and finally praying for our kiddos and for their fathers. We were just babies ourselves trying to figure out this whole motherhood thing. Through trial and error and trial and success, I watched as my friend Cathy, with grace and strength, became a mom that so many have come to look to for good advice, Godly wisdom, a shoulder to cry on and a gentle kick in the pants to just trust God with the whole matter.

The fact that all of my children are grown has not changed the fact her wisdom and love for me and my kids is as strong as ever. Parenting is one the hardest jobs in the world: so many times we don't see immediate results or compensation, but it is the most rewarding and life giving thing we as women get to do!

Straight from one mother's heart to yours, these letters will encourage, equip and engage all mothers no matter the season you find yourself in. As you read, know that prayer, tears and heart have been poured into every word.

Thanks, my friend, for your heart for mothers and for the words that will be life giving to mothers everywhere.

Ruth Mitchell
Pastor at Hillsong, Phoenix

Prologue

They say you cannot choose your family, but if I could, I would choose Cathy as my aunt again and again! I've had the privilege of knowing her for 33 years now. I know I can contact her any time with my innermost struggles to my outermost outbursts, with no judgement. And believe me, I have. She is always there with love, whether crying alongside me or rejoicing with me in victory, simply and intentionally listening and responding in words and/or directing us to God for His wisdom in prayer!

She is a true, walking testimony of a woman seeking after God - deepening her relationship with Him and her knowledge of the Word in ways that always inspire and encourage me to do likewise. I hope to be more like her as I continue to walk this journey of life.

When I first began reading these letters, I honestly could not relate much to them. I was still a new mom with only one child, and my child (besides not sleeping well, still) was an amazingly easy, happy girl! I knew we were blessed and knew we'd more than likely need these words of wisdom later on. In the meantime, I passed my first two copies of these letters to other moms, who I knew would be blessed by the wisdom and pure honesty. Something inside knew I would eventually need them for myself, so I would ask for another copy.

Then, it happened! The jump of my little girl from age 2 to 3, along with a move across country, new pregnancy, and other life changes. I found myself in a miry pit of frustrations, doubt, guilt and an ugly reality of the ugly inside me! I would write Cathy, venting, asking for prayers and pouring out my heart! I also searched for these pages, through our piles of newly moved stuff, and dove in!

To my surprise, I not only found wisdom on parenting, but I learned about myself as well! I realized that on top of these new challenges with a three year old, I was the one who needed the help on understanding my little one. As I re-read these letters, I soaked them in and realized how much I wished I had soaked in the wisdom even before this trying season. Not only for the beautiful parenting stories, wisdom and encouragements but also for my personal growth and development as a person and to be a better mom.

I also recognized, I had gone too long without daily meditating on the Word and realized how much this impacted every aspect of mine and my family's life. I was gently convicted and encouraged to jump back in at any chance I could, just as Cathy encourages and shares she did, "...I clung to God's word, and kept meditating on His truth's..." Only this would begin to bring the true, needed change in me and outflow to my family.

My aunt's open honesty was so refreshing and helped lessen my own "mom-guilt". And, it helped me to realize just how much more I needed to change my thinking! I needed to stop blaming my circumstances, a testing toddler and pregnancy emotions! "As I let God's Word get into my heart and my mind, it truly did begin to change my thinking." as Cathy wrote in Letter 1.

Cathy has always helped direct me back to God in anything and everything! This time, her words also helped me realize how crucial my relationship with God is for my daughter and raising her as He tells us to. "We are our children's first and most significant teacher in life." So humbling to realize we are not simply a "mom" who cleans messes and tries to get through the ups and downs of parenting. We are teachers, mentors, models and spiritual leaders to our children - every hour of every day. Why wait until we're in the midst of trial before seeking the wisdom

God has granted others, like Cathy? I know I will be returning to her letters time and again as we continue to walk this beautiful journey of parenting, and overall living the life God has called us to.

Michelle Edmonson
Wife, Mom, Missionary,
Ministry Travel Specialist,
Student of Life, and niece to Cathy Horning

Introduction

One thing that became clear as I prepared to write this book is that this was God's idea, long before it was mine. In fact, it's conception actually began twenty-one years ago in the midst of raising four middle and grade school age children, while attending all manner of sports, music, and youth group events, supporting my new attorney husband, and helping to run women's ministry at our church.

I remember early one morning, I woke up with a strong sense to fast certain foods for ten days. Later, when I turned on the radio in my car, I heard the host asking his listeners to fast and pray. I said out loud, "Okay, I get it, Lord!"

The next week, as I fasted and prayed, the Lord showed me where I was running ahead of Him and where I was dragging behind. Then, on the seventh day, two letters showed up in my mailbox. One came from Washington State. The other arrived from Florida, or somewhere in the southeast. Each letter was written by a friend who had moved away. Both friends were mommies to children younger than my own. Two women who had never met each other, but somehow wrote letters arriving on the same day, asking the same questions.

One friend wrote, "I am writing…to get some parenting advice… I thought of you and your family and how your kids showed so much respect for each other and for you. I remember how your kids listened without threats or yelling (she must have come over on a good day) and I really admire what I saw in your house… Do you have any words of wisdom?"

The other letter read, "I think of you so often. How great you are at being a godly mommy! (Tears, lots and lots of tears)…we are expecting again…exciting and… overwhelming… Help! How do you do it? I need your wisdom and knowledge."

I knew, this couldn't just be a coincidence! Tears poured down my cheeks, as I wondered, "how could anyone ask me about parenting?"

I knew how many times I had blown it as a mommy. God knew how much I had struggled to be the parent I longed to be. Sitting at my dining room table, I read the letters again, and cried out to God, "why are they asking me?"

It was then I noticed the grey-colored legal pad beside me. A pen rested next to it. And suddenly, the Lord began to show me things He had taught me, opening the eyes of my heart to lessons I had learned on my parenting journey. I took the pen, and began to scribble down ideas, the titles of topics I could write about and send to my precious mama friends.

For the next year and a half, before blogs and still the advent of the internet, I wrote fifteen letters, about one a month, to my two friends, and to their friends, plus a few more of my friends, and friends of their friends from all walks of life.

Then, as often happens, life got crazy, and I stopped writing the letters. From time to time, I would share copies of them, here and there. A few times, I even attempted to edit them into a parenting book. Whenever I did, however, they lost their integrity somehow, and the reality and rawness with which they were originally written lost their purity.

Then, last summer, I received this message: "My email records tell me it has been 5 years since I last emailed you, but God continues to use you in my life! I was at my wit's end with my kids and husband and cried out to God saying, 'I have tried everything to tolerate this situation…and I am out of patience—

please intervene and give me wisdom and your patience! I need your ideas and creativity for how to handle the situation.' The next day I just happened to come across the pack of letters you sent me after (my baby) was born. What a treasure those letters are!... I want to thank you again for sending those letters six years ago...I knew I would return to them when (my baby) was older and God has brought your sensitive support and maternal wisdom back to me at precisely the right moment. What a gift!"

Wow, I was in awe of how God was still using the packet of letters written all those years ago. I didn't think much more about it, until one day, while I was praying about how to best write a book idea I had for marriage, and I sensed the Lord's still, small voice saying, "You know, Cathy, you already have a book."

And I knew, it was the letters. The real, raw, unedited letters. The letters from the heart of one mother to another. The letters which now fill the pages of this book. The book, I'm pretty sure God had in mind ever since He put it on my heart to fast and pray, for those ten days, twenty-one years ago.

A mom once told me that these letters are a timeless treasure. I hope this is so! For it is my prayer for God to use them to bless and encourage you, dear Mama, as you train up, love, and raise your precious little ones for the Lord.

Letter 1

Where Did This Temper Come From?

Last Sunday, on Mother's Day, our pastor asked the mothers in the congregation to share what most surprised them about being a parent. Many special and funny thoughts were shared. I thought of things that surprised me as well, and decided to begin this series of letters by sharing one with you.

What a joyful event for my husband and me when our first child was born. I promised myself I was going to be a perfect mommy. I had read many books and taken several child development classes in preparation for motherhood.

The first surprise I encountered, as I began this new job, was that I had a temper. Where had it come from? I could only remember one time in my life when I had raised my voice at anyone. But here I was, at times, screaming at my baby. This problem was compounded for me because I had promised myself that I was never going to yell at my children.

I knew I was not the only mother surprised by her temper. Several of my friends, who are teachers, told me how they had never raised their voices at the children in their classroom, but boy, could they yell at their own kids. As I talked with and watched other moms, I found out most of them got irritated with and yelled at their children.

Reality quickly sunk in; I was not a perfect mom. However, I did not want to settle for status quo. The books I read and the classes I had taken taught it was not healthy for a child to live in a home where parents could not control their anger. And I remembered how, as a child, I hated it when adults would get angry and yell.

My second child soon arrived, and I continued to battle with my temper. I resolved with each outburst that I wouldn't let it happen again. I read books, took more classes, shed tears, and said many prayers. But, it became clear I needed more than this to help me overcome my battle with anger.

I turned more and more to God's Word. At nineteen, I had become a committed Christian and was taught early in my walk of faith to memorize Bible verses. In my desperate search to overcome my anger I looked up many verses about anger. I began to memorize these verses and pray God would teach me how to put them into practice.

I memorized James 1:19, which says, *"Everyone should be quick to listen, slow to speak, and slow to become angry."* I also memorized Colossians 3, especially the verses that talk about getting rid of anger, rage, malice... and, clothing ourselves with compassion, kindness, humility, gentleness, and patience... And, I cried out to God, "How do I do this?"

Slowly, as I clung to God's Word and kept meditating on His truths about anger and righteous living, I began to change. At first, the words I had memorized would come to mind after I would lose my temper. I would apologize to my children, again, and remind myself I needed to be quick to listen, slow to speak, and slow to become angry. Then I would pray for the Lord to forgive me and teach me His way.

A couple of years ago, after God had given me much victory in this area of my life, I was once again meditating on the verses in Colossians. I was surprised to discover the answer to my cry, "Lord, how do I do this," sandwiched between the verses on which I had concentrated. Colossians 3:9-10 read, *"since you have taken off the old self with its practices and have put on the new self, which is being renewed in knowledge in the image of its Creator."* Wow, there was the secret: to change our thinking from the old way to the new way, God's way!

As I let God's Word get into my heart and mind, it truly began to change my thinking. Instead of God's truth coming to mind after I would lose my temper, it started to guard my actions beforehand, and I had to choose whether I was going to do it God's way or my old way.

I still blow it at times. I continue, after thirteen years of parenting, to apologize to my kids and repent to the Lord when I lose my temper. I must continually remind myself of God's truth and meditate on His Word. Yet, God has answered my prayers! As His word guards my heart and mind, I learn to renew my knowledge, so I can be a mommy God's way and not my own far-from-perfect way.

As I conclude this first letter, I encourage you not to settle for the status quo mom. There is no such thing as a perfect mother, but we can seek to become excellent ones. We can renew our thinking by letting

God's word transform our hearts and minds. Let's pray for each other that the Lord will teach us to become the godly mothers He desires us to be.

No status quo mom,

Reflections

Question: What surprised you the most about being a mom?

_____

_____

_____

_____

_____

_____

_____

_____

_____

_____

_____

_____

_____

_____

_____

_____

_____

_____

_____

_____

_____

_____

Challenge: Find a scripture in the Bible to help you to renew your mind and transform your behavior in an area where you struggle as a parent.

_____

_____

_____

_____

_____

_____

_____

_____

_____

_____

_____

_____

_____

_____

_____

_____

_____

_____

_____

_____

_____

_____

_____

Letter 2

Lord, Grant Me the Patience to ~~Endure~~ Enjoy My Blessings!

On my refrigerator door, there is magnet that says, "Lord, grant me the patience to endure my blessings!" My great aunt gave it to me as a gift when my children were very small. We laughed and thought it was so cute and so fitting.

One day, at the park swimming pool with my four children, I watched the other mothers with their children, and I recalled the words on my magnet. I didn't laugh this time, because I saw that most mothers did just what the magnet said, they endured their blessings.

At home later, I took the magnet down. With a black permanent marker, I crossed out the word "endure", and I wrote above it "ENJOY"! As I wrote the word, I prayed for the Lord to teach me to enjoy my children, and not just to endure them.

There have been many circumstances in my life which could have been excuses for me to endure my blessings. I have four children close together in age, I have battled with health issues, and I felt like a single parent during the four years my husband was in law school, just to name a few.

I confess, there have been many days I have simply endured being a mother. However, I have worked to make those days the exception and not the rule. As the years go by, I can honestly say the times I endure my children are less and less, and I truly do enjoy them more and more.

In the letters to come, I hope to share with you the many lessons I have learned that have helped me to enjoy each one of my precious children. It is my fervent prayer for all mothers, as well as myself, that we will be mothers who enjoy our children, not ones who simply endure them.

Enjoying our blessings,

Cathy

Reflections

Question: If you had a magnet on your refrigerator door today, would it say you enjoy your blessings more or endure them?

_____

_____

_____

_____

_____

_____

_____

_____

_____

_____

_____

_____

_____

_____

_____

_____

_____

_____

_____

_____

_____

_____

_____

_____

Challenge: What is one action you can take to enjoy your children more?

_____

_____

_____

_____

_____

_____

_____

_____

_____

_____

_____

_____

_____

_____

_____

_____

_____

_____

_____

_____

_____

_____

_____

_____

_____

Letter 3

Get to Know Yourself and Your Kids

I'll never forget struggling to put my first born into his car seat. Tears were streaming down his face and he fought me every step of the way, as I finally snapped the last buckle.

I was late again. As I drove away, I cried out to God, "How come this child and I always clash?"

My nerves calmed, and I began to feel guilty for my harshness with my son. I apologized to him and began to pray again. Then I heard God's still small voice in my thoughts. I still remember the words, "Cathy, you do everything fast and he does things slow. I gave him to you to slow you down, and you need to warn him, at times, when you need him to speed up."

Wow, that was the truth! Taking those words to heart, I began to slow down for my son's sake. I would explain to him when we were in a hurry. And, fifteen minutes before we had to go somewhere, I would give him five-minute warnings that we were about to leave and that he needed to be ready. It was amazing how much smoother life became as I slowed down and gave him notice to speed up.

Getting to know ourselves and our kids can help us to enjoy our relationship with them, not just endure it. The revelation about the obvious contrast between how my son and I approach life helped me to see other differences in a new light. I began to study and learn about the temperaments we have and the love languages we speak.

In the next two letters, I plan to write about the different temperaments and love languages we all possess. I have found that when we recognize and work with our differences, we can enhance our relationship with our children. If we don't, we will experience strife and friction with them.

Getting to know you,

Cathy

Reflections

Question: Can you think of one area where you and your child often clash?

_____

_____

_____

_____

_____

_____

_____

_____

_____

_____

_____

_____

_____

_____

_____

_____

_____

_____

_____

_____

_____

_____

_____

_____

Challenge: Prayerfully consider how God might be using the differences between you and your child to "grow" each of you into better versions of yourself.

_____

_____

_____

_____

_____

_____

_____

_____

_____

_____

_____

_____

_____

_____

_____

_____

_____

_____

_____

_____

_____

_____

_____

_____

Letter 4

Train Up A Child In The Way He Should Go...

(...and in keeping with his individual gift or bent), and when he is old he will not depart from it. Proverbs 22:6 (AMPCE)

The moment my second child was placed in my arms, I knew he was completely different than my first born. Daniel, my first child, did not sleep through the night until he was three years old. Benjamin, my second son, slept twenty hours a day for the first six months. And through the night from a very early age.

Daniel was very cautious about trying new things. Benjamin lacked caution entirely. Daniel was clean and neat. Benjamin was like the Charlie Brown character, Pig Pen. I could have put him in a sterile

31

room and he would have found dirt. These two little boys, born to the same parents, just seventeen months apart, were as different as night and day.

Those of you who have more than one child have likely noticed that each child is very unique. If mismanaged and misunderstood, the differences can cause great conflict and competition. However, if you learn about the differences, as well as come to understand the strengths and weaknesses of your children, then you have the tools to help build a great team and a strong family.

In the book of Proverbs, we are told, "Train up a child in the way he should go…" and in the original Hebrew it actually translates to say, "according to his bent…" I love this translation as it shows clearly that God made each of our kids in a certain way, and that we need to find their unique "bent" and train them up in that way. In fact, it is extremely helpful for us to discover our own "bent," as well as that of our spouse.

A great way to learn about the "bent" our children have is to study about the four temperaments. There are many great books on this subject. My personal favorite is, "The Treasure Tree," by John and Cindy Trent and Gary and Norma Smalley.

This is a children's story book about four very different animal friends who set out on a treasure hunt. Each animal possesses a different temperament, and the strengths of each are needed to find the treasure. My children love this story to be read to them over and over. At the end of the book there is a checklist asking the children if they know what their own temperament is. It is amazing how most children are able to quickly identify the temperament they possess, often even quicker than their parents can.

The four animal friends perfectly illustrate the temperament they represent. There is the lion who wants to be the leader, and is often serious and firm. The otter is fun loving, and loves to perform and tell tales. The golden retriever is a peacemaker, who is sensitive and kind. And, finally, there is the beaver who likes routine and order, and is often honest and precise.

After reading the book to my own children the first time, I asked them what temperament they thought they had. My oldest son began to tell us that he thought he had some lion in him (usually, a person is a combination of two). Before he could finish his sentence, my youngest son roared, "You are not the lion! I am the lion!" And, with that pronouncement we knew, then and there, who was the king of our jungle.

Our family includes just about every combination of the four temperaments. As we have grown to understand our differences, we have been better able to appreciate each other and enjoy the unique ways each of us view and approach life. We have to make sure that our lions don't trample our golden retrievers. We often have to separate our otters, because their frolicking play turns into fierce fighting. And we comfort our beavers when life throws a wrench into their routine and order.

There is no way I can adequately describe the four temperaments in this letter. So, I encourage you to learn more about them and how they work in your family.

Training them up,

Books I recommend on temperaments:

The Treasure Tree[1]

The Spirit Controlled Woman[2]

---

[1] Copyright 1992© by John Trent and Gary Smalley for text
    Copyright 1992© by Judy Love for illustrations
[2] Copyright 1975© by Beverly LaHaye

Reflections

Question: Can you see signs of the different temperaments in your family?

_____

_____

_____

_____

_____

_____

_____

_____

_____

_____

_____

_____

_____

_____

_____

_____

_____

_____

_____

_____

_____

_____

_____

_____

Challenge: To the best of your ability, find out about each family members' temperament, and think of one way you can use this information to make your family stronger. (There are many online resources)

Letter 5

Fill Up Your Child's Love Tank

Two years ago, I discovered a concept called love languages, which has dramatically affected how I parent my children. Gary Chapman in his book, "The *Five* Love Languages"[3],explains that there are different ways people express love and need love expressed to them.

The five basic love languages he discovered through his counseling practice are:
Words of Affirmation
Quality Time
Gifts
Acts of Service
Physical Touch

---

[3] The *Five* Love Languages ©1992,1996,2004 by Gary Chapman

Mr. Chapman explains, although everyone needs all the languages spoken to them, each person has one, and sometimes two, primary love language(s). He found if the primary love language was not spoken to a person they develop an empty emotional love tank.

Even though the book was about marriage, it began to show me the love languages of my children. I discovered two of my children speak the love language of Gifts. These two would give away everything they owned, if I let them. My surprise was realizing that it was also the way they needed love expressed to them.

Children with Gifts as their primary love language may come across as whiney or greedy. They want you to buy them something every time you go shopping. And, they are so disappointed when you refuse to buy them something. Even at the checkout stand they are still begging you to buy anything. Gum. Candy. Baseball cards...

I don't reward begging and whining. But, as I came to understand this love language, I chose to say yes to a request, now and then. Or to secretly buy something small at the checkout counter as a surprise on the way out. To my children whose primary love language is

Gifts, this small action speaks volumes and fills up their child-sized love tank.

Remember, the child who speaks this love language, not only wants to be given gifts, but is also very generous in giving them. This child should be taught how to use their love language wisely. They need to be taught that God wants them to be generous in their giving. However, they also need to learn that people will sometimes take advantage of their generosity and that they should ask mom and dad's permission before giving things away.

Another love language is Acts of Service, which happens to be the primary love language my daughter speaks. Before I understood this, I was frustrated that she seemed to always be underfoot. She is like a little shadow, right by your side, wanting to know how it is done and if she can help.

As I began to see this love language expressed in my daughter's life, I found ways to express Acts of Service to her. She is delighted when I surprise her by doing one of her chores, or when I give her a hand with a task. I have learned to enjoy her constant presence and to let her help me more.

Another love language that Gary Chapman talks about is Quality Time. The person who speaks this love language needs one-on-one, eye-to-eye, connecting time, even if it's just a few minutes a day. This is my primary love language. I begin to wilt like a plant without water when my love language is lacking in my significant relationships.

Because this is my primary love language, it is easy for me to speak. I try to spend several minutes each day with my children individually at the end of the day. We pray together, talk and sometimes have a song or two. My husband and I also try to regularly take each child out alone on a date. They always look forward to their one-on-one time.

The love language all children need, especially when they are young, is Physical Touch. One of my gift givers also speaks this primary love language. When he was little, he loved to rub the silk edge of his baby blanket or the silky fabric on my nightshirt. He still loves to be snuggled when he wakes up in the morning and often will find me during the day, simply to get a hug.

Another one of my children speaks two primary love languages, Physical Touch and Quality Time. He has difficulty getting his homework done in a timely fashion. Needless to say, this is a great source of frustration for him and me. Since I discovered his love languages, I will go to his desk from time to time and give him a big hug and talk with him about how he is doing. Instead of scolding or threatening him, I have found that speaking his love language helps him go faster and get it done.

The last love language that Gary Chapman describes is Words of Affirmation. If a child has this as his primary love language, then the words that others speak to him carry significant weight. This child tends to shower others with kind words and praises. Be aware that many times this child may be searching for encouraging words to be spoken to him in return.

My other gift-giver also speaks the primary love language of Words of Affirmation. He is always cheering us on with verbal praise. (I keep telling him to make sure he keeps it up when he gets married). The flip side is that he is deeply affected by what others say to him, even if it is in their tone or non-verbals. This child needs daily doses of encouraging words.

Since learning about the five love languages, I have tried to be intentional to speak all five of them to each one of my children daily. Gary Chapman wrote, "when family members start speaking each other's primary love language, the emotional climate of a family is greatly enhanced." This has been true in our family.

I cannot adequately describe the love languages in this short letter. So, I encourage you to learn more about them. I believe it can be a powerful resource in your parenting, and will give you insight and understanding in all your relationships.

Overflowing in love,

Reflections

Question: What is your love language? Your child's/children's? How about your spouse?

_____

_____

_____

_____

_____

_____

_____

_____

_____

_____

_____

_____

_____

_____

_____

_____

_____

_____

_____

_____

_____

_____

_____

_____

Challenge: Think of ways you can speak the love language of your most difficult family member. Also, try to speak all 5 of them every day to every kid! (I know, big challenge. But well worth it).

Letter 6

When We Are Consistent

The admonition to be consistent is found in nearly every book I have ever read on parenting. It has caused me great guilt and anxiety. I often wondered if I damaged my children's lives by being consistently inconsistent.

Experts write that being consistent is one of the most important ingredients of parenting well. However, so many factors can cause a mother to be inconsistent. A sleepless night. That time of the month. Worry. Busyness… Just to name a few.

What a pleasant surprise when I began to see fruit in my children's lives in the areas where I had been consistent. It was such a relief, as I realized I didn't have to be consistent every minute of every day, but consistent over the weeks, months, and years.

There was such joy as I began to witness my children put into practice, without my prompting, the values, morals and manners I tried to teach them over and over again. I began to hang on to those moments, as they gave me the hope, the courage and the perseverance to keep on being consistent, and not to give up.

That said, after fourteen years of being a mommy, I also find it frustrating when I must still remind my children of the basics. We will go through seasons where I have to prompt them once again to be appreciative and to say, "thank you," or to say, "I'm sorry," even when they assure me, it was "just an accident." There are also those regular reminders to say, "excuse me" or "please." Sometimes, I think they will never learn.

Still, there are other times I see the fruit that they are learning and applying what they learn. Like when my teenage son speaks to me in a harsh tone, then catches himself, and says, "Mom, I'm sorry I spoke to you that way." Or when my little girl comes in and says, "Mommy, we have new neighbors, could I bake them some brownies and welcome them to the neighborhood?"

It brings tears to my eyes to think of the harvest I am just now beginning to reap. This harvest is not because I've been consistent every minute of every day. Believe me, I haven't. But, the harvest is because I have tried to be consistent over the weeks, months and years.

It is not easy to be consistent, but it will be worth it! Remember God's precious promise, *"Do not become weary in doing good, because you will reap a harvest if you don't give up!"* Galatians 6:9

Consistently yours,

Reflections

Question: What area do you find yourself the least consistent as a mom?

_____

_____

_____

_____

_____

_____

_____

_____

_____

_____

_____

_____

_____

_____

_____

_____

_____

_____

_____

_____

_____

_____

_____

_____

_____

_____

Challenge: Pray for the Lord to show you an area, or areas, where you are consistent. Maybe not every day, but over the weeks and months. Celebrate those areas and let them inspire you to be more consistent in the more difficult ones.

_____

_____

_____

_____

_____

_____

_____

_____

_____

_____

_____

_____

_____

_____

_____

_____

_____

_____

_____

_____

_____

_____

_____

_____

_____

_____

Letter 7

When You Blow It, Say, "I'm Sorry"

This summer was a long one for our family. My teenager has been straddling the fence between childhood and adulthood. My ten and twelve-year-old each stepped over the threshold into adolescence, and I began menopause ten years too early. Hormones have been raging, evidenced by short tempers, tears, and a lot of "I'm sorry, please forgive me."

I don't tell you this saga to make you dread adolescence or menopause. (I'll write about those topics later, when I can look back and laugh). This letter is to encourage you to apologize to your children when you blow it.

That may sound trite, but I know of parents who won't admit their failures and don't apologize to their children. They are afraid they will appear weak or perhaps lose their children's respect. However, I believe the very opposite is true.

It is essential for children to hear the words, "I'm sorry, will you please forgive me?" when you overreact or say something wrong or mess up. When your children hear these words, they will learn at least three valuable lessons.

First, your children will learn that you are not perfect and that you don't think that you are. They will see that Mom is human and that she makes mistakes and blows it sometimes, just like they do.

Next, your children will learn what is right and what is wrong. When they hear you say, "I'm sorry," at those times when you have blown it, they will learn that those behaviors, attitudes and words are wrong.

Finally, your children will learn to admit when they are wrong and to repent. They will see, through your example, the times when an apology is necessary. They will learn to say, "I'm sorry, please forgive me," when they overreact or say something wrong or when they just plain blow it.

If you are honest and humble and ask your children to forgive you, you will be laying the very foundation to teach them about repentance and forgiveness. 1 John 1:8-9 says, *"If we claim to be without sin, we deceive ourselves and the truth is not in us. If we confess our sins, He is faithful and just and will forgive us our sins and purify us from all unrighteousness."*

We must instill in our children the need for repentance and forgiveness; it's importance in their own life, in their relationship with others, and in their relationship with God. We need to teach them to ask for forgiveness and to grant forgiveness. Remember, we are modeling to our children the powerful act of repentance and forgiveness.

*On a side note, there are parents who say, "I'm sorry" too often. I am a peacemaker, so I tend to apologize even when I'm not at fault. If you, like me, are a person who says, "I'm sorry," too much, think about when and why you apologize. Work on <u>not</u> saying, "I'm sorry," when you really have not done anything wrong. And, look for ways to reword your sentences. For example, instead of saying, "I'm sorry you don't like it," perhaps say, "I know you don't like this, maybe we can find something you do like."

With love and forgiveness,

Cathy

Reflections

Question: Do you ever find it difficult to tell your kids you blew it, or to simply confess a wrong (as a model to them)? When you do confess, what does that look like? When you do, do you find it helpful to mend a rift between you and your child(ren) and to restore peace?

_____

_____

_____

_____

_____

_____

_____

_____

_____

_____

_____

_____

_____

_____

_____

_____

_____

_____

_____

_____

Challenge: Think of a true story to tell your children about a time you got in trouble as a kid, then confessed it, and were granted grace and forgiveness. Or, perhaps, think of the opposite, a time when you got in trouble, tried to hide or lie about it, and then the guilt and burden you carried from it, and possibly the trouble you got into later when you were found out.

Letter 8

Raise Up a Standard

If you were to imagine a measuring stick for parenting, beginning with lenient and ending with strict, my husband and I would measure on the strict end. Our children, who are now old enough to be aware of this, know that our rules and boundaries differ from many of their friends.

Recently, I had to tell my oldest son that he couldn't go to a movie that "everyone else was going to see." As he wandered off, obviously disappointed, I was overwhelmed with the thought that our strict boundaries could cause our children to rebel someday. I went to my knees in prayer and asked the Lord for wisdom.

I clearly heard the still small voice of God speak to me, "Raise up a standard." Immediately I understood God was showing me that even if my children did rebel, by raising up a standard for them now, they would know what to come back to later. This small phrase, "Raise up a standard," renewed my courage to parent according to my convictions.

Recently, we had an interesting dinner conversation about this very subject. One of our children asked why we were stricter than many families they knew. We went around the table and they shared with us the areas where our rules and boundaries were different than others they spent time with.

Our children proceeded to discuss the rigid guidelines we have for television and movie viewing. They brought up the fact that they are not allowed to raid the refrigerator or pantry anytime they want. They complained about the "early" bedtime hour we enforced, which turned into a discussion about respect, and how we required it from them towards everyone, especially each other.

As the conversation ended, our children decided our rules and boundaries were a good thing. They realized it helped clarify for them what was right and wrong. They also understood that they were learning how to draw and set boundaries in their own lives.

It is difficult, as parents, to set rules and boundaries which are contrary to what "everybody else is doing." However, I believe with all my heart that we must "raise up a standard" for our children. As they grow up that standard will be in their heart. It will be a measure for them to live up to and it will be there to convict them should there ever be a season of rebellion.

As we raise up a standard,

Cathy

Reflections

Question: What is a standard that you have in your home, especially one that seems contrary to what "everybody else is doing it?"

_____

_____
_____
_____
_____
_____
_____
_____
_____
_____
_____
_____
_____
_____
_____
_____
_____
_____
_____
_____
_____
_____
_____

Challenge: Find a Bible passage to hold on to in regards to an area that is particularly hard to tow-the-line on.

_____

_____

_____

_____

_____

_____

_____

_____

_____

_____

_____

_____

_____

_____

_____

_____

_____

_____

_____

_____

_____

_____

Letter 9

The Black, White, and Grey of Setting Boundaries

I received a phone call a couple of weeks ago from a mom who was encouraged by my last letter on *Raising Up a Standard.* She explained to me how both she and her husband had been raised with few boundaries, and she was now finding it difficult to set them for her own child.

Like this precious mom, I too have found it incredibly difficult to set boundaries and raise up a standard for my children. From the time our first child was born, it has been my husband who is strong in this area. For him things are clearly black and white, right and wrong, good or bad. On the other hand, I have had huge grey areas of what is permissible.

When our children were very young, this was a great source of conflict for me. On the drive home from the hospital with our first born, my husband insisted that our crying newborn ride all the way home in his car seat. I had assumed I would take him out and hold him or feed him if he were upset. (This was before stringent car seat laws).

As our family grew and other conflicting issues would arise, I quickly began to learn that my husband's seemingly strict and "uncompassionate" rules were actually a source of great wisdom, love and security for our children. At the same time, it became obvious that there was more testing, strife, and confusion when the rules were within my wide grey areas.

In addition to the example my husband has been in my life, there has been even a greater resource I continually turn to as I strive to raise up a standard for my children. That resource is God's Word. As I have learned what the Bible says about how we are to live our lives, I have been able to make rules and set boundaries that are not only my idea, but God's.

Taped above our television for several years hung a paper that read, *"I will set no worthless thing before my eyes."* Psalm 101:3 (NASB) My children and their friends routinely hear me say, "this is not just my rule, this is God's rule." They know that the standard we raise up for them is not just something we make up ourselves.

Recently, my son was reading the small Bible I carry in my purse as we drove to an appointment. He suddenly exclaimed, "Mom, you know how you and dad are so strict?"

"Yes," I answered, smiling inside, because I knew he had not read my last letter about this topic.

He continued, "well listen to this, *'Whoever loves discipline, loves knowledge, but he who hates reproof is stupid.'"* (Proverbs 12:1) He was very impressed with this verse and it confirmed to him, that according to God's Word, his parents were on the right track.

Were you raised without boundaries, like the mom I referred to above? Or, like myself, is setting boundaries a big grey area for you? If so, find out what God's Word says about these areas. Also, pray for and seek out other moms who can model parenting skills where you may be weak.

Learning the fine art of boundary setting,

Reflections

Question: Are boundaries a pretty black and white area for you? Or, are they more grey?

_____

_____

_____

_____

_____

_____

_____

_____

_____

_____

_____

_____

_____

_____

_____

_____

_____

_____

_____

_____

_____

_____

_____

_____

_____

Challenge: Think of an area where you kids know they can push your buttons. Prayerfully consider a plan of action you can implement next time they try to wear you down. (For me, a simple truth I needed to remind myself was, "I am the mom!)

_____

_____

_____

_____

_____

_____

_____

_____

_____

_____

_____

_____

_____

_____

_____

_____

_____

_____

_____

_____

_____

_____

_____

_____

Letter 10

The Best Book on Parenting

One of the friends who originally asked me to write about parenting also requested I recommend any good books on the subject. As you know, I have done just that in past letters and will recommend others in the future.

This letter, however, is devoted to recommending a book that not only has given me insight and knowledge into parenting, but has also transformed my life. I have referred to this book often in my previous letters. It is God's Word, the Bible.

Although I went to church as a child, I was never encouraged or taught to read my Bible until I became a young adult. Once I began to read and study God's Word, I loved spending time in it every day. My life began to change dramatically as I discovered God's plan for my life.

As I studied the Word of God, rebellion turned into surrender, pain into peace, despair into hope, anger into love, and fear into faith. I discovered in the pages of the Bible the very words of God that bring life, healing and restoration.

Once I had children, I found that spending time in the Bible was nearly impossible. The times when I did read it regularly, there would be growth and good fruit in my life. But, when I slacked off, I would be stagnant with little or no growth. In Matthew 4:4, Jesus says, *"Man does not live on bread alone, but on every word that comes from the mouth of God."* I realized I was starving for God's Word.

Until recently, it was a constant struggle to squeeze Bible reading into my day. I tried to wake up before the children, but I'm convinced they heard the light switch click on, because as soon as I began to read the first verse, I would hear their good morning greeting. Over time, because I knew the great value of consistently being in God's Word, I learned little secrets to help me feast upon it more often.

I realized many times I found the time to read and watch other things. So, I made a commitment to myself that I would read God's Word before anything else…newspaper, television, good books, etc.

I even discovered times where I actually had a few moments alone, usually while waiting at a doctor or dentist appointment. There on the table next to me sat all those enticing magazines. So, I began to carry a small Bible with me. If I had not spent time in God's Word that day, out would come my Bible. I was able to feed myself on the Word of God, instead of the latest gossip.

The most valuable secret I learned was to memorize Bible verses. I would write verses on 3x5 cards and put them near the sink where I could see them while I did the dishes. I would also carry them in my purse, and read them over and over for days, until I had them memorized.

Psalm 1 says, *"Blessed is the man who does not walk in the counsel of the wicked, nor stand in the path of sinners, nor sit in the seat of scoffers. But his delight is in the law of the Lord, and on His law he meditates day and night. He is like a tree firmly planted by streams of water, which yields its fruit in its season, and it's leaf does not wither. And, in whatever he does, he prospers."* (NASB)

I believe that memorizing scripture is the most powerful way to "mediate on God's word day and night," because you have it inside you. Once God's

Word begins to work in your heart it cannot help but transform and change your life. Psalm 119:11 says, *"I have hidden your word in my heart, that I might not sin against you."*

As I close, I encourage you, Mom, to read your Bible and to hide God's Word in your heart. It is the most valuable book you can have in your library. God's Word is a classic on parenting, and it is guaranteed to change your life from the inside out.

Parenting according to God's Word,

Cathy

Reflections

Question: For most moms, especially with little ones, finding time to be in the Bible is hard. No guilt here, but do you have a Bible? Do you open it up? Do you read it? Would you like to try to spend more time in God's Word?

_____

_____

_____

_____

_____

_____

_____

_____

_____

_____

_____

_____

_____

_____

_____

_____

_____

_____

_____

_____

_____

_____

Challenge: Ask the Lord, and/or a friend, how to best spend time in God's Word in this season of life. (I truly believe there is an extra measure of grace to sustain mommies with simple snatches of the Word when their children are small). Use a phone app, a paper version (one with a pretty cover, a pleasing font, and a version you enjoy), a devotional, or perhaps, an audio version. It requires discipline and dedication, but begin a regular reading time. If you don't know where to begin, may I suggest the gospel of Mark, the Proverbs, or Psalms.

_____

_____

_____

_____

_____

_____

_____

_____

_____

_____

_____

_____

_____

_____

_____

_____

_____

Letter 11

Planting God's Word in Their Hearts

How can a young man keep his way pure? By living it according to your word." Psalm 119:9 ESV

We are our children's first and most significant teacher in life. As such, I believe one of the most valuable things we can teach our children is to know the Word of God. Last month, I encouraged you, dear Mom, to read your Bible and to make it a priority in your day, every day; to feast on the "bread of life." Now, I would like to challenge you to pass this invaluable discipline on to your child.

There are many wonderful ways to teach children the Word of God. Christian bookstores are full of cassette tapes and C.D.'s which put scripture to song. In addition, there are a wide array of Children's Bibles and Family Devotionals. Your children may also enjoy the many Bible games that are available.

75

Our family tried many methods and materials to teach our children God's Word. I know of families who have a devotion every day. I confess, we have never been successful at making this habit for more than a few weeks at a time. When I homeschooled my children, we attempted to memorize verses every week. However, I usually felt a lot of guilt for my lack of consistency.

What a surprise one day, when driving somewhere with my children, I realized the most effective and powerful way I was teaching them about God's Word was according to His instructions to us in Deuteronomy 11:18-19. *"Fix these words of mine in your hearts and minds... Teach them to your children, talking about them when you sit at home and when you walk along the road, when you lie down and when you get up."*

I recalled all the conversations we had about God and His Word in the natural course of everyday life. Many of the most incredible lessons I have been able to teach my kids have literally been "as we walked along the road," (or in our case, drove).

As my children learn about the Word of God in real life context, it is not uncommon for one of them to remind us of God's Word at a fitting moment. For example, after something has gone very wrong, we are often reminded of Romans 8:28, *"And we know that in all things God works for the good of those who love Him, who have been called according to His purpose."*

Just last week, God's Word worked powerfully in the heart of my son. He had an argument with his older brother, there were unkind words and slammed doors. Then later, while reading his Bible, he came across the verses in James about keeping a "tight rein on your tongue," plus, "being quick to listen, slow to speak, and slow to become angry." He was so convicted, on his own, he went and apologized. Wow, I didn't even have to get involved.

We are raising our children in very scary times. This past week alone, has been full of tragic stories. What an awesome privilege and responsibility we have as our children's most significant teachers who can plant God's Word within their hearts. How can our children keep their way pure? "By living according to Your Word."

Planting good seeds,

Cathy

Reflections

Question: Does God's Word have an everyday, normal place in your home?

_____

_____

_____

_____

_____

_____

_____

_____

_____

_____

_____

_____

_____

_____

_____

_____

_____

_____

_____

_____

_____

_____

_____

_____

_____

Challenge: Teach your kids to hide God's Word in their heart early. There are many wonderful kids apps and bible resources on line and in stores. Early on, I began putting down Bible verses on a big piece of poster board and we would memorize that verse each week. Also, when they were afraid or needed God's promise about something, we would write a verse on a 3x5 card and keep it under their pillow. Even before they could read this was a great comfort to them. Now my grandchildren do it as well.

_____

_____

_____

_____

_____

_____

_____

_____

_____

_____

_____

_____

_____

_____

_____

_____

_____

_____

Letter 12

Get Down on Your Knees and Pray

"But when you pray, go into your room, close the door and pray to your Father, who is unseen. Then your Father, who sees what is done in secret, will reward you...for your Father knows what you need before you ask Him." Matthew 6:6-8

Last week, a friend and I were sharing stories of a time when each of our daughters, as infants, battled spinal meningitis. Thankfully, each little girl recovered, but tears filled my eyes, as we recounted the anxious memories. Then my friend turned to me and said, "I bet you never prayed harder."

Instantly, I remembered times when I prayed just as hard, and all of them were situations which involved the life of my children. I have found that nothing will bring a mother to her knees quicker than when one of her children is hurt, sick, or in danger.

81

I love the story in 1 Samuel 1:10-20 of Hannah "pouring out her soul to the Lord" for a child she did not yet have. Certainly, there is nothing more powerful, passionate or pleasing to the Lord than a mother's prayers for her children!

How vividly I remember the first time I was aware of the power of a mother's prayers. At the age of eleven, I was involved in a serious car accident. It was my first trip away from home without my family. Very late at night, on the long drive across Arizona, our fast-moving car collided with a cow.

As the police pried the doors open to get us out, I realized it was a miracle that I was still alive. I had been kneeling on the console between the two front seats, when just seconds before the collision, something prompted me to move on to the floor behind the driver's seat. Had I stayed where I was, the impact would have ejected me from the car and I would have been killed or seriously injured.

Later, I would find out that my mother had been praying for me for hours. She felt uncomfortable about my going on the trip from the beginning, but she passed it off, not wanting to be over-protective. However, when the feeling did not go away, my mom went to her "prayer closet" and literally prayed for me the whole time, until she received the phone call about the accident.

I am thankful my mother listened to the Spirt of God within her and for the prayers she said for me. Romans 8:26 says, *"The Spirit helps us in our weakness. We do not know what we ought to pray for, but the Spirit Himself intercedes for us with through wordless groans."*

My life was forever impacted that night, as I witnessed the answer to my mother's fervent prayers for me. I was convinced, even at that young age, God had spared my life for a reason.

Years later, after my graduation from high school, I began to see the passion of mother's prayers. I moved out on my own, and for the next two years I ran away from God and my faith. At first, my mom tried to convict me of my rebellion with her words, but soon her words stopped. Instead, she just loved me and prayed for me.

During this dark season, I was well aware of my mother's prayers. As she watched my life spiral downhill, she must have wondered if God was answering her. Later, she would discover God indeed was answering her prayers. Through the consequences of my wrong choices, God was drawing me back to Himself. I am sure my mother's prayers also protected me from far worse consequences.

I am eternally grateful for the power and the passion of my mother's faithful prayers in my life. I believe nothing is more pleasing to the Lord than when we, as mothers, acknowledge our dependence upon Him and our need for His help in raising our children. He longs to help us take care of the precious gifts He has given to us. We just need to ask.

I hope when our children grow up, they will look back and know the power and the passion of a praying mom. I know they will see the difference in their lives and I believe the Lord will be pleased that we were mothers on our knees.

On bended knee,

Cathy

Reflections

Question: Do you pray for your children? When do you pray? How do you pray?

_____

_____

_____

_____

_____

_____

_____

_____

_____

_____

_____

_____

_____

_____

_____

_____

_____

_____

_____

_____

_____

_____

_____

Challenge: If you're not already doing this, pick one time a day to pray (out loud) for your child. On the way to school, at a meal, before bedtime. The Lord loves for us to come to Him in prayer, and it can be an honest, simple, open conversation just like with a very trustworthy friend. To go a step further, our kids loved to keep a prayer journal. Usually in the evening, when we prayed together as a family, we would write down our prayers in a notebook. Our kids had no greater joy than recording the answer to those prayers, along with the date, and to see what God had been up to.

_____

_____

_____

_____

_____

_____

_____

_____

_____

_____

_____

_____

_____

_____

_____

_____

Lesson 13

Teaching Our Children to Pray

"This is the confidence we have in approaching God; that if we ask anything according to His will, He hears us. And we know that He hears us—-whatever we ask—-we know that we have what we asked of Him." 1 John 5:14-15

I have heard when baby birds are ready to fly, the mother bird will push them out of the nest to help get them started. At the ripe old age of twenty, my mother also "pushed me out of the nest." Of course, my shocking shove was not to teach me to fly, but how to pray!

I remember my childhood bedtime prayer, "Now I lay me down to sleep, I pray the Lord my soul to keep…" And, our mealtime prayer consisted of "God is great, God is good. Let us thank Him for our food."

I said other prayers too, in the quiet of my heart. Usually, pleas for help or petitions for things I wanted.

It was not until I became a young adult that I began to realize the power of prayer. However, because of the season of rebellion I went through in my teens years, I felt unworthy for God to listen to my prayers. This dilemma led me to call my mom whenever I needed prayer for anything. I knew God heard and answered her prayers.

One day, when I called home to enlist the prayers of my mother, I received quite a shock. My mom told me not to call her anymore with my prayer requests. This wise woman informed me that she knew the reason I called her was because I didn't believe God would listen to my prayers. She explained to me how she wanted me to learn that God heard and would answer the prayers I said, just as He answered hers.

It has been nearly twenty years since my mother "pushed me out of the nest," and I have learned God does hear and answer my prayers. That firm and loving shove has also inspired me to teach my own children to pray, and for them to know that God will hear and answer their prayers.

Teaching our children to pray and teaching them God's Word (as I wrote in a previous letter) are just as crucial to their survival and success in this world as a mama bird teaching her babies to fly. From the time my children were infants I have taught them that they can talk to God anytime, anywhere and about anything.

I have tried to instill in my children the truth that God is always with them, even when I am not. And, that He will never leave them or forsake them. (Hebrews 13:5) My children have learned they can talk to God anytime. We pray at bedtimes and mealtimes, in the middle of the night when they have had bad dreams or in the middle of the day when someone has gotten hurt, in trouble, or just had a rough day.

We also pray anywhere, not just in our home or at church. We often pray in our car on the way to school, a sports activity, or a friend's house. At times we have stopped in a small huddle to say prayers in a restaurant, at a store, at a park, or anywhere we happen to be when we need divine intervention. We even pray over the phone.

More important than when or where they pray, I want my children to learn that they can pray about anything. We serve a God who knows what we need before we ask (Matthew 6:8), and yet He wants us to come to Him, to have a relationship with Him. So, I have tried to teach my children that they can go to God about everything.

Many of the petitions sent heavenward, daily, in our family are asking for help to find a shoe, or a baseball glove, or a backpack. I tell my children, God knows where it is, so ask Him to put the thought in your head where to look. It is amazing, and sometimes downright miraculous, how things show up.

I also encourage my children to pray for God's wisdom with homework problems. I know God may use me to help them find the answer, but I won't always be there to help, and I want them to learn to go to God first! Besides, He always knows the answer; sometimes I don't. It has been absolutely faith building for all of us to watch the Lord answer those prayers and give my children the wisdom they need for almost all their homework questions.

We really do pray for everything, from the smallest issues of tummy aches and finding lost items, to the larger issues of future spouses and what God made each child to do and be. We pray anywhere we happen to be, not just at the dinner table or at bedtime. And we pray anytime, because we know that God is always right there with us, waiting for us to call upon Him.

My children see evidence every day that prayer is powerful, and they know God does hear and answer their prayers. They are learning they can talk to God anytime, anywhere, and about anything. I believe that teaching our children to pray is as essential as a mama bird teaching her babies to fly.

As we teach our children to pray,

Reflections

Question: Do you model a prayer relationship with the Lord to your children? If you're new to this, learn with them. Let them know, just like they can come to you, they can ask God for anything, anytime, anywhere, and that He can send even greater answers than mom and dad.

_____

_____

_____

_____

_____

_____

_____

_____

_____

_____

_____

_____

_____

_____

_____

_____

_____

_____

_____

_____

_____

_____

Challenge: Before you help your child find something missing or with a homework problem or with the answer to something they're wanting, ask them to pray about it first. God may use you to help with the answer, but teach them to go to God, who loves them even more than you do!

Letter 14

Breaking Out of The Guilt Trap

Recently, I took the day off from my normal "mom" duties to drive up the coast to Santa Monica. There I spent the day with a friend from my college days, and had the joy of meeting her new baby boy. My friend waited thirty-six years for this child, and I was in awe as I watched her care for her new son. I knew she was going to be a great mom.

We caught up on the highlights of the past years. Then, our conversation naturally turned to child-rearing. We talked at length about all the differing "expert" opinions. Should you put them on a schedule, or feed them on demand? Do you let them sleep with you, or make them sleep in their own bed? And what about diapers, bottles, pacifiers, and, oh don't forget, discipline?

My friend confessed to me that each day, in her short three months of parenthood, she felt overwhelmed with guilt that she might be doing "it" wrong. I was surprised by her confession, for she appeared so calm and confident. But at the same time, I knew exactly how she felt. Every mom I know, myself included, wrestles constantly with this strong emotion.

I am convinced there is nothing that can rob, and even extinguish, the joy of motherhood quite like guilt. I can remember the awful feeling of guilt each time I discovered I was pregnant. I would question if I had consumed any food or drink or medication that could have harmed the baby. Or had I done any potentially dangerous activity, like moving heavy furniture.

If the guilt we feel when they are babies isn't enough, our precious children quickly learn we possess this emotion. At a young age, they master just what "buttons to push" to get this emotion to kick in for their advantage. Before long, mom can become worn out from a never-ending battle with guilt.

A "button" my children quickly came to recognize was that I hate to tell them "no." Needless to say, my four children have gotten a lot of mileage out of this button. However, as I have grown in my parenting skills and, quite frankly, grown tired of feeling guilty, I am learning to have victory over this enemy.

I will never forget that first time I recognized I had won the battle over the "button pushing." The kids and I were on the way home from an afternoon at the beach. As we drove past a large, grassy park, my son passionately reminded me that I had promised him we would fly his new kite. He pleaded with me to stop at the wide open spot, on what happened to be a particularly windy day.

I held my ground, and informed my son we had already had a full day and we would not be stopping. In my mind, I convinced myself that this was the right and best decision for our family. And, I reminded myself, I was the boss. I looked over at my son, who looked heartbroken and on the verge of tears. For perhaps the first time, I felt no guilt! I was not shaken, and I stood my ground.

When my son saw my resolve and how his tactic had not worked, we both burst into a roar of laughter. He tried to gain his composure, but his bluff had been called. I felt such freedom as I took control and stuck to my decision. I also caught a glimpse of the ability I had given my children to steer my emotions.

Romans 8:1-2 says, *"There is now no condemnation for those who are in Christ Jesus, because through Christ Jesus the law of the Spirit who gives life has set me free from the law of sin and death."* When I found this passage of scripture, I was so relieved to see that God knows we try to do our best. He knows we won't do it perfectly, but we can rest in His perfect work in our lives.

As we seek to do our best, it is also a great comfort to know the Lord promises to help us any time we ask. James 1:5 says, *"If any of you lacks wisdom, you should ask God, who gives generously to all without finding fault and it will be given to you."*

God does not want us to waste our days battling with emotional guilt. He wants us to enjoy raising our children in the freedom He gives us as we follow His expert advice. We can rest in God's promises that we are free from condemnation, that He knows we are doing our best, and that He will give us His wisdom, generously, whenever we ask.

Guilty no more,

Reflections

Question: What do you find causes you the most guilt as a mom?

_____

_____

_____

_____

_____

_____

_____

_____

_____

_____

_____

_____

_____

_____

_____

_____

_____

_____

_____

_____

_____

_____

Challenge: When you find yourself struggling under the weight of mom guilt, ask the Lord to help you. (God is not the one who heaps guilt upon his kids. Yes, there will be conviction in our hearts if there is something we need to change or work on to be a better mom, but not guilt and shame.) Be very careful what you are reading and listening to, who you are comparing yourself with, and the self-talk you are beating yourself up about. Find someone, a family member, friend or even a counselor who will speak life-giving truth, in love, to you. Learn to recognize futile thoughts, and ask the Lord to help you to dwell on what is right and true and up lifting.

_____

_____

_____

_____

_____

_____

_____

_____

_____

_____

_____

_____

_____

_____

_____

Letter 15

Make Time for One-on-One

Last Sunday afternoon, I sat across the table from my fourteen-year-old son at the local Hard Rock Cafe, where we shared a basket of french fries and icy cold Cokes. We discussed the restaurants memorabilia, old rock stars, and music. As we sat there, enjoying each other's company, I realized it had been a long time since I had spent purposeful time alone with my oldest.

I recalled, years ago, when I discovered my second child was on the way, how I had purposed in my heart to regularly spend time alone with each one of my children. Over the years, they have come to look forward to their date with mom or dad. The dates are specially planned to let our children have our undivided time and attention, usually doing something they particularly enjoy.

A good friend of mine recently shared with me her favorite childhood memory. She was about ten, when her mother decided to spend one hour alone with each of her four children. The hour was spent doing whatever that particular child wanted. My friend remembers playing Monopoly one week, and bicycle riding another. When she shared this fond memory with her mom, she learned the plan only lasted about one month, but what an impact that one month made in my friend's life.

This summer, my husband, who often works long hours, decided he wanted to spend more time with our kids. He came up with a plan he calls, "Breakfast with Dad." Four mornings a week, he has breakfast alone with each one of our four children. While they eat breakfast, they talk, pray, and study the Bible together for about half-an-hour. My children look forward to their morning alone with their dad, and my husband has enjoyed getting to know our kids even better during this special one-on-one time.

The past three months, I have watched my children grow closer to their dad as he has purposed to spend time alone with each of them, even in the midst of a very demanding career. It is evident to me, from watching my children with their dad and from the story my friend remembers, that one of the most precious gifts we can give our children is one-on-one time. Sipping sodas and sharing french fries with my teenage son at the Hard Rock Cafe reminded me that no matter how old our kids get, they're never too old for our undivided attention, just to talk, to listen and to laugh.

When they are grown, what will our children remember as some of their favorite memories? Will they have warm thoughts of times when we gave them our undivided attention? I hope and pray we will be moms who purpose to set aside time to nurture each one of our children individually, as well as in our family setting.

One-on-one,

Cathy

Reflections

Question: Do you spend one-on-one time with each child? How often are you able to make that happen?

_____

_____

_____

_____

_____

_____

_____

_____

_____

_____

_____

_____

_____

_____

_____

_____

_____

_____

_____

_____

_____

_____

_____

_____

_____

_____

Challenge: Whether it is once a week or once a month, plan a way to spend one-on-one time with each child. Most kids don't really care when and where, they are just satisfied with your undivided attention.

_____

_____

_____

_____

_____

_____

_____

_____

_____

_____

_____

_____

_____

_____

_____

_____

_____

_____

_____

_____

_____

_____

_____

Letter 16

Twenty Years Later

My friend, and the founder of The MOM Initiative, Stephanie Shott[4] writes, "Motherhood is a fluid journey that doesn't end the day our children turn that magical age of 18. You're their mom for life - and you will always be their biggest cheerleader and most relentless prayer warrior. No one will ever want as much for your children as you do and no one will ever pray for them like you will. So, keep on cheering, keep on praying, and rest in the beautiful truth that God loves them even more than you do!"

I really had no idea, or plan, that the fifteenth letter, Make Time for One-on-One, would be the last. But life got crazy, and here it is twenty-one years later. My children are all grown up, and Stephanie's words

---

[4] Stephanie Shott Bible Teacher, Author, and Founder of The MOM Initiative, To Know Him and Make Him Known
www.themominitiative.com
www.stephanieshott.com

absolutely ring true. Dearest Mama, you will never stop cheering them on. You will always pray them through. And, after you have done all that, you will only experience true rest in the truth that God lavishly loves your children (young or old) even more than you do.

Much has changed in our world from the time I wrote these letters, especially technology. That said, there is not much I would change about the messages I wrote. But, there is much I would add. So, I will write this final letter with just a few more thoughts.

One of the most valuable pieces of advice I would offer, in addition to keeping God's Word and prayer as a daily priority in your life and the lives of your children, is to surround yourself and your family with a community of friends and mentors.

Over the years, I have made wonderful mom friends. I met them at church, in my neighborhood, through school activities and sports events, at parks and coffee shops, and now online. I watched, listened to, confided in, prayed for and with, and learned all I could from those mom friends, as well as from the experienced older women in my life. And I prayed, and continue to pray, for the Lord to send friends, mentors, teachers, role models, coaches, and wise counselors into my adult children and grandchildren's lives too.

I still believe learning about the love languages and temperaments, as well as other components like birth order, learning styles, and the strengths and talents of our family, are invaluable resources in discovering how to live and love each other better. Yet, I have learned that these qualities can evolve, change, and become more clear over time as our children grow and mature. Plus, these helpful tools are not excuses for any of us to get away with or to get out of difficult relationships or circumstances of life. In fact, these attributes are often the very conduit God uses for our character development and growth. And, while they help us know ourselves and our children better, we need to be careful that they never limit us or define us in an unhealthy way.

Finally, twenty-one years later, I can clearly see that even though my friends and I all parented a little (or a lot) differently, we each did the very best we knew how with the family God entrusted to us. Most of us traveled down some rough patches, and went through some tough seasons, but all-in-all our kids have grown up to be very remarkable men and women. And as you come to your own hard seasons, which you will, I implore you to keep the faith! To pray! To seek the

Lord with all of your heart! To cling to His promises and hold fast to the truths in God's Word, and to surround yourself with a supportive community.

You, dear Mom, are doing a great job! Better than you know or can imagine! You are the perfect one who God chose to be your kids' parent. God knows you! He knows your husband! He knows each child. And He promises, *"If any of you lacks wisdom, you should ask God, who gives generously to all without finding fault, and it will be given to you."* James 1:5

Cheering you on, dear mama!
In His Love and Grace,

Reflections

Question: Do you have a life-giving community surrounding you?

_____

_____

_____

_____

_____

_____

_____

_____

_____

_____

_____

_____

_____

_____

_____

_____

_____

_____

_____

_____

_____

_____

_____

Challenge: I went through two seasons of loneliness when my children were young. Both times God used it to teach me many things. Two of the biggest lessons I learned were to depend more on the Lord and that I needed to learn to be a better friend. Each time, I also cried out to God to send mentors and friends. And He did. It didn't happen overnight, either time, but when it happened it turned into a harvest I still enjoy today. So, my final challenge for you is to pray for, and to seek out, the community of friends and mentors God would have you to be surrounded by. And, to make sure you are a contributing member of that community, as well.

About the Author

Cathy Horning is an author, speaker, Bible study teacher, blogger, and mentor who loves to encourage women, wives, and mamas on their faith journey. In addition to spending as much time as possible with her husband, grown up children, and nearly a dozen grandchildren, she is currently working on her next book, *"I Do Will," Falling in Love Again and Again.* You can find more of the stories Cathy has written and the lessons she has learned on her website at www.cathyhorning.com

Connect with us today to
ORDER BOOKS or to
INVITE CATHY
TO SPEAK
at your next event.

#1 Best Selling Author,
Speaker, Blogger

CathyHorning.com
Cathy@CathyHorning.com

Made in the USA
San Bernardino, CA
12 July 2018